REAL LIFE MATH

fly a JUMBO jet

**Wendy Clemson, David Clemson,
and Chris Perry**

Ticktock

This library edition published in 2014 by Ticktock
First published in the USA in 2013 by Ticktock,
an imprint of Octopus Publishing Group Ltd

Distributed by Black Rabbit Books
P.O. Box 3263, Mankato, MN 56002

With thanks to our consultants: Jenni Back and Liz Pumfrey from the NRICH Project,
Cambridge University, and to Kerry Johnson, Debra Voege and Lorna Cowan.

Cataloging-in-Publication Data is available from the Library of Congress
ISBN 978 1 78325 195 7

Printed and bound in China

1 3 5 7 9 10 8 6 4 2

WENDY CLEMSON

Wendy is experienced in working with and for children, and has been writing full-time since 1989. Her publications, which now exceed one hundred, have been written for children and sometimes their parents and teachers. In her many math books, the aim is always to present the reader with challenges that are fun.

DAVID CLEMSON

David has wide-ranging experience as a writer and educationalist. His publications list is prodigious. In collaboration with Wendy, David has worked on many math books for children. He is fascinated by math and logic puzzles and is eager for the reader to enjoy them, too.

CHRIS PERRY

Chris is a qualified pilot and instructor. He works at the Oxford Aviation Training College in England, teaching prospective pilots to fly a wide range of aircraft, including commercial airliners, such as the Boeing 747-400 – the jumbo jet.

CONTENTS

MATH SKILLS COVERED IN THIS BOOK:

CALCULATIONS:
Throughout this book there are opportunities to practice **addition, subtraction, multiplication,** and **division** using both mental calculation strategies and pencil and paper methods.

NUMBERS AND THE NUMBER SYSTEM:
- COMPARING & ORDERING NUMBERS: pgs. 6, 18
- FRACTIONS: pgs. 10, 14
- READING NUMBERS IN WORDS AND FIGURES: pg. 6

SOLVING "REAL LIFE" PROBLEMS:
- CHOOSING THE OPERATION: pgs. 8, 10, 12, 14, 16, 18, 21, 22
- MEASURES: pgs. 11, 12, 14, 16, 18, 22, 25
- TIME: pgs. 12, 17, 21, 22

HANDLING DATA:
- BAR GRAPHS: pgs. 8, 24
- USING TABLES/CHARTS/DIAGRAMS: pgs. 6, 8, 10, 11, 12, 18

MEASURES:
- RELATIONSHIPS BETWEEN UNITS OF MEASUREMENT: pg. 25
- USING MEASUREMENTS: pgs. 6, 10, 11, 12, 14, 16, 17, 18, 21, 22, 23, 25
- VOCABULARY (time): pgs. 14, 16, 17, 22, 23, 24

SHAPE AND SPACE:
- 2-D SHAPES: pg. 27
- 3-D SHAPES: pg. 15
- COMPASS DIRECTIONS: pg. 12
- GRID COORDINATES: pg. 26

Supports math standards for ages 10+

HOW TO USE THIS BOOK

Math is important in the lives of people everywhere. We use math when we play a game, ride a bike, go shopping – in fact, all the time! Everyone needs to use math at work. You may not realize it, but a pilot uses math to fly a jumbo jet! With this book you will get the chance to try lots of exciting math activities using real life data and facts about planes and the work of airline pilots. Practice your math skills and experience the thrill of what it's really like to fly a jumbo jet.

This exciting math book is very easy to use – check out what's inside!

Fun-to-read information about airliners and the work of airline pilots.

THE AMAZING JUMBO JET

You have reached the rank of first officer, and you are now an experienced pilot. Today, you will be flying the fastest **commercial airliner** in service – the Boeing 747-400, or jumbo jet. This amazing plane flies at MACH .85 – this means it flies at 85 percent of the speed of sound. A jumbo jet's tail is about the same height as a six-story building, and its wings are so large that 45 cars could park on them! Pilots have to arrive at the airport at least 80 minutes before a flight to carry out their preflight preparations. Start your preparations by taking your PILOT ASSESSMENT.

MATH ACTIVITIES

Look for the
PILOT ASSESSMENT.
You will find real life math activities and questions.

To answer some of the questions, you will need to collect data from a DATA BOX. Sometimes, you will need to collect facts and data from the text or from charts and diagrams.

Be prepared! You will need a pen or pencil and a notebook to figure out the answers.

PILOT ASSESSMENT

Before a flight, one of the pilots must walk around the plane making a detailed series of checks. This is called a *walk-around*. Make some checks on your plane by working out these **fractions** and divisions. Use the jumbo jet information in the DATA BOX.

1) One-third of the tires on the plane's wheels need replacing. How many is that?

2) How many ladders, seven feet tall, have to be joined together to reach the top of the plane's tail?

3) Four workers are cleaning the insides of the plane's windows. How many do they each clean?

4) The plane's fuel tanks are half full of fuel. How many more gallons of fuel are needed to fill the plane's tanks?

5) How many in-flight magazines are needed for all of the passenger seats?

(You will find TIPS to help you with these questions on page 28.)

The maintenance crew checks the jumbo jet's tires and engines.

DATA BOX

If you see one of these boxes, there will be important data inside that will help you with the math activities.

MATH ACTIVITIES

Feeling confident? Try these extra **CHALLENGE QUESTIONS.**

JUMBO JET FACT

Every 747-400 has 6,000,000 (six million) parts, 5 miles of tubing, and a massive 170 miles of wiring!

DATA BOX **BOEING 747-400**

Maximum takeoff mass (weight)	875,015 lb.
Operating empty mass (weight)	399,480 lb.
Maximum **fuel capacity**	57,280 gal. (372,880 lb.)
Average fuel burn	4,850 lb./hr per engine
Maximum **range**	8,355 **statute miles** (sm)
Typical **cruising speed**	570 mph
Jet engines	4 x 61,820 lb. thrust*
Engine cowling (outside covering)	8.5 ft. diameter
Dimensions	211 ft. **wingspan**
	231 ft. overall length
	64 ft. tail height
Total number of windows	188
Total number of wheels	18
Crew	5 flight deck crew
	17 **cabin** crew (flight attendants)
Passenger capacity	Standard 3-class arrangement:
	34 first-class passengers
	76 business-class passengers
	302 economy-class passengers

Thrust is the amount of force a plane's engines can deliver.

CHALLENGE QUESTION

Carry out a *walk-around* of a 747-400. Walk from the aircraft's nose to the wings, along under one wing, and then back. Then walk under the other wing and back. Finally, walk to the tip of the tail.

Approximately how far have you walked?

(Use the plane's measurements in the DATA BOX.)

PILOT FACT

Here are some of the checks that pilots need to make during their *walk-around*:
• Check that there are no dead birds trapped inside the engines.
• Check that the **fuselage** skin is in an acceptable condition and that the tires are not worn.
• Make sure that the lights on the wings, flaps, and tailfin are working.

11

IF YOU NEED HELP...

TIPS FOR MATH SUCCESS

On pages 28–29 you will find lots of tips to help you with your math work.

ANSWERS

Turn to pages 30–31 to check your answers.
(Try all the activities and questions before you take a look at the answers.)

GLOSSARY

On page 32 there is a glossary of aviation words and a glossary of math words. The glossary words appear **in bold** in the text.

Fun-to-read facts about planes and flying.

5

LEARNING TO FLY AN AIRLINER

Trainee pilots are called cadets. They learn to fly using **flight simulators.** Cadets have to sit examinations and spend 200 hours flying real planes before they can graduate. To become a pilot you need to study **aerodynamics, navigation**, radio communication, and even **meteorology.** All the training is worth it though, because there are some amazing planes out there just waiting to take off! During their careers, pilots learn to fly lots of different aircraft. Today, you are in the flight simulator. Look at the question on the clipboard and take your CADET PILOT ASSESSMENT.

CADET PILOT ASSESSMENT

In the DATA BOX you will see information about four **commercial airliners**. Use the information to figure out which aircraft has been programmed into the flight simulator for your training flight.

(You need to compare the aircraft.)

- It has a **wingspan** that is less than the wingspan of the Boeing 777.
- It has a **range** greater than the Airbus A320.
- It is third largest in order of tail height.
- It is smallest in order of takeoff mass (weight).
- It has engines with approximately 22,700 lb. thrust.

Which aircraft is programmed into the flight simulator?

(You will find information about UNITS OF MEASUREMENT on page 29.)

CHALLENGE QUESTION

Which of these is the maximum **fuel capacity** of the Airbus A320?
a) Six thousand three hundred and thirty gallons
b) Six thousand three hundred and three gallons
c) Six thousand and thirty-three gallons

(You will find a TIP to help you with this question on page 28.)

FLIGHT TRAINING FACT

Flight simulators are machines that use computer programs to create flying conditions just like the real thing. Pilots use flight simulators to practice taking off and landing, and to practice dealing with **turbulence**, thunderstorms, and emergencies, such as an engine failure!

Airbus A320

Max. takeoff mass (weight)	162,050 lb.
Maximum fuel capacity	6,303 gal.
Maximum range	3,050 **statute miles** (sm)
Typical **cruising speed**	530 mph
Jet engines	2 x 23,830 lb. thrust*
Dimensions	112 ft. wingspan
	123 ft. overall length
	38 ft. tail height

Airbus A340

Max. takeoff mass (weight)	607,300 lb.
Maximum fuel capacity	40,960 gal.
Maximum range	9,200 statute miles (sm)
Typical cruising speed	555 mph
Jet engines	4 x 32,600 lb. thrust
Dimensions	197 ft. wingspan
	195 ft. overall length
	54 ft. tail height

Boeing 737

Max. takeoff mass (weight)	143,500 lb.
Maximum fuel capacity	6,900 gal.
Maximum range	3,510 statute miles (sm)
Typical cruising speed	530 mph
Jet engines	2 x 22,705 lb. thrust
Dimensions	112 ft. wingspan
	102 ft. overall length
	41 ft. tail height

Boeing 777

Max. takeoff mass (weight)	660,000 lb.
Maximum fuel capacity	45,220 gal.
Maximum range	6,850 statute miles (sm)
Typical cruising speed	560 mph
Jet engines	2 x 94,640 lb. thrust
Dimensions	200 ft. wingspan
	242 ft. overall length
	60 ft. tail height

Thrust is the amount of force a plane's engines can deliver.

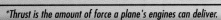

Airline pilots are able to fly into any airport in the world. They use special charts, called Jeppesen Charts, that show them the length and width of the runways and details about the height and location of any mountains or tall buildings in the area. Today, you are the second officer (the junior pilot) on a flight to Atlanta, Georgia. Your plane is about to land at Hartsfield International Airport – the busiest airport in the world! Over 44,800 people work at Hartsfield, and flights take off and land 24 hours a day. It is now time to take your SECOND OFFICER ASSESSMENT.

SECOND OFFICER ASSESSMENT

In the DATA BOX you will see the enormous numbers of passengers that go through the world's busiest airports every year. The passenger numbers for six of the airports have been put into a **bar graph**, but the airport name labels are missing.

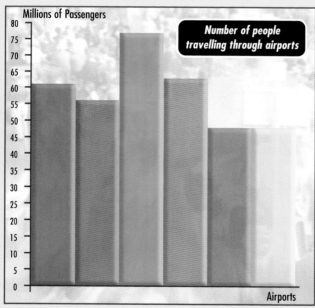

Millions of Passengers

Number of people travelling through airports

Airports

Which bar stands for which airport?

(To get you started, the red bar stands for the number of passengers going through Los Angeles International Airport.)

(You will find TIPS to help you with this activity on page 28.)

CHALLENGE QUESTION

If you wanted to know how many passengers went through each of the airports in a week, what would you need to do?

(You will find a TIP to help you with this question on page 28.)

DATA BOX WORLD'S TOP 10 BUSIEST AIRPORTS

Number of passengers per year:

1st Hartsfield International, Atlanta, USA	77,000,000
2nd O'Hare International, Chicago, USA	67,000,000
3rd Heathrow Airport, London, UK	63,000,000
4th Haneda International, Tokyo, Japan	61,000,000
5th Los Angeles International, Los Angeles, USA	56,000,000
6th Dallas Fort Worth International, Dallas, USA	53,000,000
7th Frankfurt Airport, Frankfurt, Germany	48,000,000
8th Charles de Gaulle International, Paris, France	48,000,000
9th Schiphol International, Amsterdam, Netherlands	41,000,000
10th Denver International, Denver, USA	36,000,000

Hartsfield International Airport viewed from a plane.

Concorde lands at Heathrow Airport for the last time in October 2003.

THE AMAZING JUMBO JET

You have reached the rank of first officer, and you are now an experienced pilot. Today, you will be flying the fastest **commercial airliner** in service – the Boeing 747-400, or jumbo jet. This amazing plane flies at MACH .85 – this means it flies at 85 percent of the speed of sound. A jumbo jet's tail is about the same height as a six-story building, and its wings are so large that 45 cars could park on them! Pilots have to arrive at the airport at least 80 minutes before a flight to carry out their preflight preparations. Start your preparations by taking your PILOT ASSESSMENT.

PILOT ASSESSMENT

Before a flight, one of the pilots must walk around the plane making a detailed series of checks. This is called a *walk-around*. Make some checks on your plane by working out these **fractions** and divisions. Use the jumbo jet information in the DATA BOX.

1) One-third of the tires on the plane's wheels need replacing. How many is that?

2) How many ladders, eight feet tall, have to be joined together to reach the top of the plane's tail?

3) Four workers are cleaning the insides of the plane's windows. How many do they each clean?

4) The plane's fuel tanks are half full of fuel. How many more gallons of fuel are needed to fill the plane's tanks?

5) How many in-flight magazines are needed for all of the passenger seats?

(You will find TIPS to help you with these questions on page 28.)

(You will find TIPS to help you with these questions on page 28.)

The maintenance crew checks the jumbo jet's tires and engines.

DATA BOX ▸ BOEING 747-400

Maximum takeoff mass (weight)	875,015 lb.
Operating empty mass (weight)	399,480 lb.
Maximum **fuel capacity**	57,280 gal. (372,880 lb.)
Average fuel burn	4,850 lb./hr per engine
Maximum **range**	8,355 **statute miles** (sm)
Typical **cruising speed**	570 mph
Jet engines	4 x 61,820 lb. thrust*
Engine cowling (outside covering)	8.5 ft. diameter
Dimensions	211 ft. **wingspan**
	231 ft. overall length
	64 ft. tail height
Total number of windows	188
Total number of wheels	18
Crew	5 flight deck crew
	17 **cabin** crew (flight attendants)
Passenger capacity	Standard 3-class arrangement:
	34 first-class passengers
	76 business-class passengers
	302 economy-class passengers

*Thrust is the amount of force a plane's engines can deliver.

PILOT FACT

Here are some of the checks pilots need to make during their *walk-around*:

- Check that are no dead birds trapped inside the engines.
- Check that the **fuselage** skin is in an acceptable condition and that tires are not worn.
- Make sure that the lights on the wings, flaps, and tailfin are working.

CHALLENGE QUESTION

Carry out a *walk-around* of a 747-400. Walk from the aircraft's nose to the wings, along under one wing, and then back. Then walk under the other wing and back. Finally, walk to the tip of the tail.

Approximately how far have you walked?

(Use the plane's measurements in the DATA BOX.)

MAKING A FLIGHT PLAN

One of the most important preflight jobs that a pilot does is prepare a **flight plan.** Today, your airline wants you to fly from Heathrow Airport in London to John F. Kennedy Airport (JFK) in New York City. The flight plan will show important information about the flight, such as how much fuel will be used, the speed that the plane will travel at, the direction of the wind, and how long the flight will take. The information in the flight plan will be input into the plane's computer system. You will need to use times and distances to complete your next PILOT ASSESSMENT.

PILOT ASSESSMENT

The map and DATA BOX on these pages show the types of information that pilots use to help them plan their flights. Using the travel times and distances in the DATA BOX, work out the answers to these questions:

1) How much further is it from Paris to Cairo than from Moscow to Rome?

2) What is the difference in journey time between New York to Los Angeles and Los Angeles to Atlanta?

3) You are planning to fly from London to Cairo via Paris. What is the distance that you will travel?

You are flying from London to Atlanta, via New York and Los Angeles.

4) How far will you travel?

5) What is the total travel time?

(You will find a TIP to help you with questions 2 and 5 on page 28.)

CHALLENGE QUESTIONS

Use the compass on the map to answer the following questions:

a) Which cities on the map are SW of Washington, D.C.?
b) Which city on the map is NE of Rome?
c) Which cities on the map are southeast of Paris?

Los Angeles

Atlanta

FLIGHT FACT

Pilots are trained to fly around the world using *air corridors* – imaginary roads in the sky.

JUMBO JET FACT

Between them, all the 747s in service have flown 35 billion miles. That's enough miles to make 74,000 trips to the Moon and back!

DATA BOX · FLIGHT TIMES AND DISTANCES

Journey	Distance	Travel time
London to New York	3,444 miles	6 hours
New York to Boston	186 miles	30 minutes
New York to Washington, D.C.	228 miles	45 minutes
New York to Los Angeles	2,471 miles	4 hours 30 minutes
Los Angeles to Atlanta	1,944 miles	3 hours 40 minutes
London to Paris	216 miles	23 minutes
Paris to Cairo	2,363 miles	4 hours 15 minutes
Moscow to Rome	1,893 miles	3 hours 30 minutes

During their preflight preparations, pilots must calculate how much fuel they will need for the journey. A jumbo jet has an incredible **cruising speed** of 570 mph. At this speed, the plane's four engines will burn approximately 19,800 lb. of fuel every hour. The average car would have to drive at top speed, nonstop day and night, for over a month, to use as much fuel as a jumbo jet uses in one hour! All aircraft must carry enough fuel to reach their destination, as well as some spare fuel in case there is an emergency, and the flight is diverted to another airport. Before you fly, you will need to check how much fuel is needed for your journey.

PILOT ASSESSMENT

- *You will be flying a jumbo jet, which burns 19,800 lb. of fuel per hour.*

- *It will take 6 hours to get from Heathrow Airport, London, to JFK Airport, New York City.*

1) How many pounds of fuel are needed?

- *If there is an emergency at JFK, you may be diverted to an airport in Boston or Washington, D.C.*

2) If you divert to Boston airport, you will need fuel for a further half-hour. How many pounds of fuel is that?

3) If you divert to Washington, D.C., you will need fuel for an extra three-quarters of an hour. How many pounds of fuel is that?

A tanker delivers fuel to a jumbo jet.

*A view of the **cockpit** in a jumbo jet*

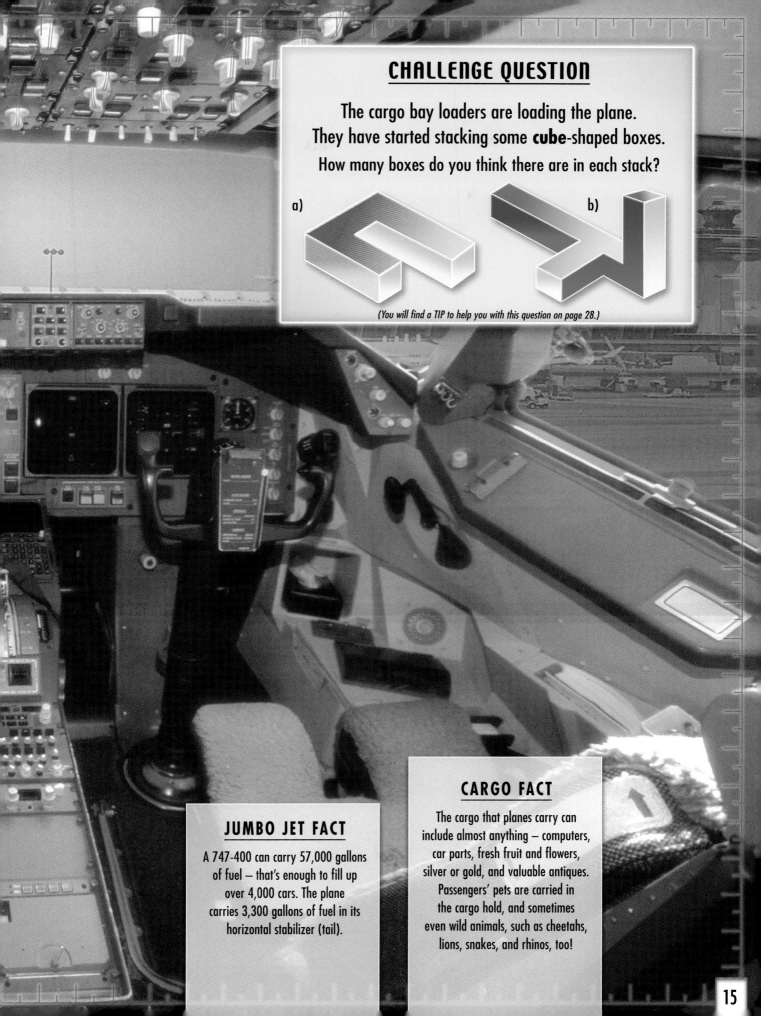

CHALLENGE QUESTION

The cargo bay loaders are loading the plane.
They have started stacking some **cube**-shaped boxes.
How many boxes do you think there are in each stack?

a)

b)

(You will find a TIP to help you with this question on page 28.)

CARGO FACT

The cargo that planes carry can
include almost anything – computers,
car parts, fresh fruit and flowers,
silver or gold, and valuable antiques.
Passengers' pets are carried in
the cargo hold, and sometimes
even wild animals, such as cheetahs,
lions, snakes, and rhinos, too!

JUMBO JET FACT

A 747-400 can carry 57,000 gallons
of fuel – that's enough to fill up
over 4,000 cars. The plane
carries 3,300 gallons of fuel in its
horizontal stabilizer (tail).

Working as a team with the captain, you have filed your **flight plan**, calculated your fuel, examined the weather forecasts, and checked your aircraft — both the outside of the plane and the **flight instruments** in the **cockpit**. You are now sitting in the right-hand seat in the cockpit. Both pilot seats have the same controls, but today, the captain is PNF (pilot nonflying). This means you are the PF (pilot flying) — you will be flying the plane! There is one more PILOT ASSESSMENT to work through before takeoff.

PILOT ASSESSMENT

The most your aircraft and its contents can weigh at takeoff is 875,015 lb. You must not overload your plane!

- *The empty plane weighs 399,480 lb.*
- *You have filled up with 147,710 lb. of fuel.*

1) What is the weight of the empty plane and its fuel?

2) What is the maximum that the cargo, passengers, and crew can now weigh?

- *When your plane takes off, it will climb 3,000 ft. every minute.*

3) How high will you be after 5 minutes?

4) How high will you be after 10 minutes?

5) After 12 minutes, the plane levels out. What is the plane's altitude (height above ground level)?

A 747-400 taxis onto the runway.

Airliners wait in a line to be cleared for takeoff.

Leaving the ground

LANDING PROCEDURE

- The captain tells the crew to prepare for landing.

- The captain and copilot run through the landing briefing. This includes all the normal procedures and the actions to be taken if there is an emergency.

- The wing flaps and undercarriage (wheels) are lowered.

- The control tower at the airport clears the aircraft to land.

- Once the aircraft has passed over the runway threshold, the **thrust** levers are pulled back and the nose is lifted by pulling back on the controls. This makes sure that the plane lands on the stronger, main undercarriage.

- As a jumbo jet touches down, it is travelling at 160 mph.

- The brakes will reach temperatures of 392°F as they stop the plane!

- Welcome to Washington Dulles Airport.

PILOT FACT

Pilots are only allowed to fly for eight *flying hours* in a day, 100 *flying hours* in a month, and 1,000 *flying hours* in a year. Flights that are longer than eight hours are called *long-haul flights*.

CHALLENGE QUESTIONS

It takes 6,740 feet for a plane to stop on a dry runway, and an extra 1,180 feet if the runway is wet.

a) What is the wet runway stopping distance?
b) Now write your answer in miles, and then in inches.

(You will find information about UNITS OF MEASUREMENT on page 29.)

You are now in Washington, D.C. You have flown a total of 3,672 miles and your aircraft has burned over 20,605 gallons of fuel. In an average car this would be enough fuel to drive from the Earth to the Moon, back to the Earth, and then back to the Moon again! While you are making your postflight report, you have one final PILOT ASSESSMENT to try. Pilots must be able to read maps and charts. Can you find things at the airport using a grid map and coordinates?

It has been a pleasure flying with you, and we look forward to flying with you again.

PILOT ASSESSMENT

There are lots of things happening at Washington Dulles Airport.

1) Your plane is on the runway. What are the coordinates of its nose?

2) What things can be found at these coordinates: (1,2) (4,3) (2,1) (1,4)?

3) What are the coordinates of the passenger bus?

(You will find TIPS to help you with these questions on page 29.)

CARGO FACT

The NOTAC (Notification to Captain) is a document that tells the captain about any special or dangerous cargo that may be on board.

CARGO FACT

The 747-400 is so well designed that airline cargo handlers can unload 66,000 pounds of cargo in under 15 minutes. That's about 33 **tons** of freight and 625 pieces of luggage!

Cargo can be loaded and unloaded through a jumbo jet's nose.

CHALLENGE QUESTIONS

The baggage handlers have a number of packages to unload. The ends of the packages are different shapes.

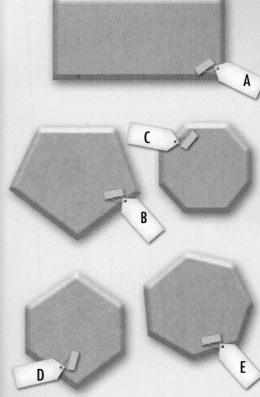

a) Name the shape that has four **right angles**?
b) Name the shape that has two pairs of sides of equal length?
c) Which **regular** shape can be made from six identical **equilateral triangles**?
d) Find the shapes with seven and eight sides. What are they called?
e) In which shape can you join all of the corners to make a star with a **pentagon** in its center?

TIPS FOR MATH SUCCESS

PAGES 6–7

CHALLENGE QUESTION
Reading and writing large numbers:

TIP: When reading or listening to the names of large numbers, such as:

fifteen thousand eight hundred and six

it helps to write the number using numbers like this: *15,806*

PAGES 8–9

SECOND OFFICER ASSESSMENT
Interpreting a bar graph:
It is the heights of the bars in a **bar graph** that allow you to compare things.

In a bar graph you need to know what the scale is. For example, is the scale going up in 1s, 2s, 5s, 10s, 100s, 1,000s, or some other amount?

Bar graphs should always have a title.

You need to know what each bar stands for, too.

The heights of the bars on the bar graph on page 8 show the numbers of passengers. If the red bar is Los Angeles International Airport, then you know that this bar shows 56,000,000. Look at the heights of the other bars and match them to the numbers of passengers in the DATA BOX.

CHALLENGE QUESTION
TIP: There are 52 weeks in a year.

PAGES 10–11

PILOT ASSESSMENT
Understanding division:
Fractions and division are related. For example, finding one-half of a thing or a number is the same as dividing it by two.

If you know a multiplication fact, then you also know some other related facts. For example: **15 x 4 = 60** and from this we know that **60 ÷ 15 = 4**

PAGES 12–13

PILOT ASSESSMENT
TIP: There are 60 minutes in one hour.

PAGES 14–15

CHALLENGE QUESTION
Imagining 3-D shapes:
TIP: If you find it difficult to imagine the shapes made by the stacks of **cube**-shaped boxes, get some small blocks and try making the shapes.

PAGES 16–17

CHALLENGE QUESTIONS
Calculations:
TIP: Before doing any calculation, decide what sort of calculation it is: *addition, subtraction, division, or multiplication?*
For example, if a plane travels 300 miles in one hour, and you need to find out how far it travels in one minute, you need to *divide* 300 by 60 (minutes).

PAGES 18–19

PILOT ASSESSMENT
Comparing numbers:
Here are the meanings for the symbols:
> means more than   < means less than

For example:
16 – 3 > 99 – 95
¼ < 0.5

KLM

PH-BXS

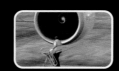

PAGES 22–23

PILOT ASSESSMENT

TIP: If you are going to circle New York City, you need enough fuel for 2 hours 5 minutes of flight.

Using a 24-hour clock:

Airlines use a 24-hour clock to avoid confusion between a.m. and p.m. Look at the analog clocks. In 24 hours (a day and a night), the hour hand travels twice around the clock face.

ANALOG CLOCKS	DIGITAL CLOCKS

06:00

6 a.m. or 6:00 a.m.

18:00

6 p.m. or 6:00 p.m.

• six o'clock

03:30

3:30 a.m.

15:30

3:30 p.m.

• Half past three
• Three thirty

TIP: "a.m." means before noon (in the morning) and "p.m." means after noon.

PAGES 24–25

PILOT ASSESSMENT

A **bar graph** uses bars to show information. To read a bar graph you need to look at the tops of the bars and the scale at the side to find out where the bars reach.

PAGES 26–27

PILOT ASSESSMENT

Using coordinates:

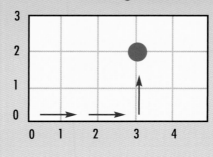

To find the coordinates of a point on a grid, you read along the bottom of the grid first and then up the side of the grid.

For example, a grid reference of **(3,2)** means **3 steps** along the bottom and then **2 steps** up to find the exact point.

UNITS OF MEASUREMENT

There are two systems of measurement. The customary system uses inches, feet, miles, ounces, and pounds. The metric system uses centimeters, meters, kilometers, grams, and kilograms.

METRIC		CUSTOMARY	
Length		**Length**	
1 millimeter (mm)		1 inch (in.)	
1 centimeter (cm)	= 10 mm	1 foot (ft.)	= 12 in.
1 meter (m)	= 100 cm	1 yard (yd.)	= 3 ft.
1 kilometer (km)	= 1,000 m	1 mile	= 1,760 yd.
Weight		**Weight**	
1 gram (g)		1 ounce (oz.)	
1 kilogram (kg)	= 1,000 g	1 pound (lb.)	= 16 oz.
Capacity		**Capacity**	
1 milliliter (ml)		1 fluid ounce (fl. oz.)	
1 centiliter (cl)	= 10 ml	1 pint (pt.)	= 16 fl. oz.
1 liter (l)	= 1,000 ml	1 gallon (gal.)	= 8 pt.

Comparing metric and customary measurements:

1 kilometer = 0.62 of a mile
1 kilogram = 2.2 pounds
0.47 liter = 1 pint

ANSWERS ANSWERS ANSWERS

PAGES 6-7

CADET PILOT ASSESSMENT

The aircraft programmed into the **flight simulator** is the Boeing 737.

CHALLENGE QUESTION

b) Six thousand three hundred and three gallons (6,303 gallons)

PAGES 8-9

SECOND OFFICER ASSESSMENT

The **bar graph** shows the following numbers of passengers:

- Blue bar: 61,000,000 Haneda International
- Red bar: 56,000,000 Los Angeles International
- Green bar: 77,000,000 Hartsfield International
- Pink bar: 63,000,000 Heathrow Airport
- Purple and yellow bars: 48,000,000 Frankfurt Airport or Charles de Gaulle International

CHALLENGE QUESTION

You would need to divide the passenger numbers by 52 to find out how many passengers go through each airport in a week.

PAGES 10-11

PILOT ASSESSMENT

1) 6 tires need replacing.
2) 8 ladders
3) Each worker cleans 47 windows.
4) 28,640 gallons
5) 412 in-flight magazines are needed.

CHALLENGE QUESTION

You have walked 653 ft.

The length of the plane	231 ft.
Twice the **wingspan** (2 x 211 ft.)	+ 422 ft.
	653 ft.

PAGES 12-13

PILOT ASSESSMENT

1) 470 miles further
2) 50 minutes difference
3) You will travel 2,579 miles.
4) You will travel 7,859 miles.
5) The total journey time is 14 hours and 10 minutes

CHALLENGE QUESTIONS

a) Atlanta and Los Angeles   b) Moscow

c) Rome and Cairo

PAGES 14-15

PILOT ASSESSMENT

1) 118,800 lb. of fuel
2) 9,900 lb. of fuel
3) 14,850 lb. of fuel

CHALLENGE QUESTION

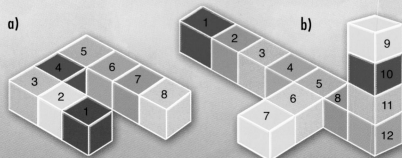

PAGES 16–17

PILOT ASSESSMENT

1) The weight of the plane and fuel is 547,190 lb.
2) The maximum that the cargo, passengers, and crew can weigh is 327,825 lb.
3) After 5 minutes, you will be 15,000 ft. high.
4) After 10 minutes, you'll be 30,000 ft. high.
5) After 12 minutes, the plane's altitude is 36,000 ft.

CHALLENGE QUESTIONS

a) 7 miles in one minute
b) 84 miles in 12 minutes

PAGES 18–19

PILOT ASSESSMENT

1) 371 bottles
2) 1.5 quarts
3) 99 cartons
4) 5 quarts
5) 28 bottles
6) True
7) True
8) False

CHALLENGE QUESTIONS

a) 4 pots of tea
b) 6 quarts of water

PAGES 20–21

CHALLENGE QUESTIONS

a) 2 hours
b) 11:00 p.m.
c) Half an hour (30 minutes) longer
d) 11:30 p.m.

PAGES 22–23

PILOT ASSESSMENT

Option 3: Fly to Washington Airport is the correct choice.

(Option 1 is wrong because you would need just over 39,600 lb. of fuel to circle for 2 hours and 5 minutes. Option 2 is wrong because Boston Airport closes in 20 minutes and it will take you 30 minutes to fly there.)

CHALLENGE QUESTION

You would need 49,500 lb. of fuel to fly (circle) for two and a half hours.

PAGES 24–25

PILOT ASSESSMENT

1) 21,000 ft.
2) 2 minutes
3) 12,250 ft.
4) 7,001 ft.
5) 09:04

CHALLENGE QUESTIONS

a) The wet runway stopping distance is 7,920 ft.
b) 1.5 miles, 95,040 inches

PAGES 26–27

PILOT ASSESSMENT

1) (5,1)

2) (1,2) Fire engine
   (4,3) **Control tower**
   (2,1) Fuel tanker
   (1,4) Plane taking off

3) (3,2)

CHALLENGE QUESTIONS

a) The rectangle (shape A) has four **right angles**.

b) The rectangle has two pairs of sides of equal length.

c) The **regular** hexagon (shape D) can be made from six identical **equilateral triangles**.

d) Seven sides (shape E) = heptagon
Eight sides (shape C) = octagon

e) You can join all the corners of a **pentagon** (shape B) to make a star with a pentagon in its center.

GLOSSARY

AERODYNAMICS The study of how solid things move through the air.

AIR TRAFFIC CONTROLLERS People who work in air traffic control. ATCs make sure that planes stay a safe distance apart in the sky. ATCs inform pilots about the weather and other problems and they organize the flow of planes in and out of airports.

CABIN Where the passengers sit in an aircraft.

COCKPIT The area at the front of the plane where the pilots sit.

COMMERCIAL AIRLINERS Planes that carry people or cargo for money.

CONTROL TOWER The airport building where the air traffic controllers work.

CRUISING SPEED A steady, constant speed that a plane flies at when it has reached its flying level.

FLIGHT INSTRUMENTS The mechanical and electrical devices used for flying a plane.

FLIGHT PLAN A detailed plan of a plane's journey, showing where the plane will fly, the length of the flight, how much fuel will be used, the plane's speed, and the expected weather conditions.

FLIGHT SIMULATORS Machines that use computer programs to create real life flying conditions. Pilots train and practice in flight simulators.

FUEL CAPACITY The amount of fuel a plane can carry.

FUSELAGE The central body section of a plane.

METEOROLOGY Studying weather.

NAVIGATION Working out the best route for an aircraft to take.

RADAR A method of detecting distant objects or weather using radio waves.

RANGE The distance a plane can fly without refuelling.

STATUTE MILES The official way of saying "miles." Pilots use this term.

THRUST A pushing force created in a jet engine, giving the plane enough speed to take off.

TURBULENCE Strong currents of rising and falling air. Turbulence can make a flight bumpy.

WINGSPAN The distance between the tips of the wings of an aircraft.

MATH GLOSSARY

BAR GRAPH A graph with bars of the same width that can be used to compare numbers of things against a scale. The height of the bar can be read against the scale on the graph.

CUBE A regular 3-D shape with six square faces.

EQUILATERAL TRIANGLES Triangles with all three sides equal in length.

FRACTIONS A fraction is a part of a whole. The bottom number of a fraction (denominator) tells how many parts the whole is divided into. The top number (numerator) tells how many parts of the whole you are referring to. If a shape is divided into four equal parts, each part is ¼ (one-quarter) of the whole.

PENTAGON A 2-D shape with five sides.

REGULAR Used to describe 2-D shapes that have sides equal in length and 3-D shapes with faces all the same in shape and size.

RIGHT ANGLE A quarter of a whole turn or revolution, measured in degrees. A right angle is 90 degrees (90°).

TONS A unit of measurement. One ton is 2,000 pounds.

VOLUME The amount of space something takes up or how much it holds — for example, the amount of liquid a bottle holds.

t=top, b=bottom, c=center, l=left, r=right, OFC=outside front cover, OBC=outside back cover

Alamy: 10bl, 14-15main. BAA Aviation Photo Library: 10br, 14bl, 16c.
Dean Barnes (AirTeamImages): 18-19main. Corbis: 12-13. Tony Decker: 27. Steve Dreier: 16t.
Daniel Hamer: 9b. Joe Pries Commercial Aviation Photography: 23tc. Andy Jung: 8-9main. John Kelly: 10-11. Will Lanting: 22-23main.
Garry Lewis (ATCO Aviation photography): 1, 2, 3, 7, 16b, 17, OBC. John Powell: 24-25, OBC. Shutterstock: 24 bc. The Flight Collection: 18c. Ticktock Media: 23bc.

Every effort has been made to trace the copyright holders, and we apologize in advance for any unintentional omissions.
We would be pleased to insert the appropriate acknowledgements in any subsequent edition of this publication.